TEMPERATURE

REVISED AND UPDATED

Measuring the Weather

Alan Rodgers and Angella Streluk

Heinemann
LIBRARY

www.heinemann.co.uk/library

Visit our website to find out more information about Heinemann Library books.

To order:

☎ Phone 44 (0) 1865 888066

▤ Send a fax to 44 (0)1865 314091

▢ Visit the Heinemann Library Bookshop at www.heinemann.co.uk/library to browse our catalogue and order online.

First published in Great Britain by Heinemann Library, Halley Court, Jordan Hill, Oxford OX2 8EJ, part of Harcourt Education.
Heinemann Library is a registered trademark of Harcourt Education Ltd.

Editorial: Joanna Talbot
Design: Michelle Lisseter and Philippa Jenkins
Picture Research: Ruth Blair
Production: Julie Carter

Originated by Chroma Graphics
Printed and bound in China by South China Printing Company Limited

ISBN 978 0 431 03852 0
12 11 10 09 08
10 9 8 7 6 5 4 3 2 1

British Library Cataloguing in Publication Data
Rodgers, Alan
 Temperature. - (Measuring the weather)
 1.Temperature - measurement - Juvenile literature
 I. Title II. Streluk, Angella
 551.5'25
A full catalogue record for this book is available from the British Library.

Acknowledgements
The publishers would like to thank the following for permission to reproduce photographs: A McLure (The Met Office) p. **4**; Alamy/Chuck Eckert p. **11**; Corbis/Kul Bhatia/zefa p. **16**; Eye Ubiquitous p. **16**; Getty images/Science Faction p. **20**; Geoscience Features p. **19**; Robert Harding Picture Library p. **12**; Science Photo Library pp. **9**, **10** (Jerry Mason), **14**, **27** (NASA); The Met Office/Crown p. **18**; Trevor Clifford Photography pp. **6**, **7**, **8**, **13**, **23**, **25**.

Cover photograph reproduced with permission of Tudor Photography and Photodisc.

Our thanks to Jacquie Syvret of the Met Office for her assistance during the preparation of this book.

Every effort has been made to contact copyright holders of any material reproduced in this book. Any omissions will be rectified in subsequent printings if notice is given to the publishers.

Disclaimer
All the Internet addresses (URLs) given in this book were valid at the time of going to press. However, due to the dynamic nature of the Internet, some addresses may have changed, or sites may have changed or ceased to exist since publication. While the author and publishers regret any inconvenience this may cause readers, no responsibility for any such changes can be accepted by either the author or publishers.

Contents

You can find words in bold, **like this**, in the Glossary.

Temperature and the weather

We all feel the effects of hot and cold temperatures, but are we aware of the effect that the temperature has on the weather in general? How can we tell exactly how hot or cold it is? There is a lot to learn about measuring the temperature.

The weather reports that we see on the television, in newspapers, and on the Internet come from professional **meteorologists.** They carefully take measurements of the weather from all around the world. Meteorologists all take measurements in the same way, so that they can swap **data.** This helps the meteorologists to build up a picture of the weather around the world. This data is also very useful for local weather forecasters. A good knowledge of how the weather behaves in one area can help weather forecasters predict what it will be like each day. The changes in temperature are part of a day's experience of weather. In some places, the weather is similar every day, all year round. In other places, the weather is different for each season. **Climate** is the weather over a long period of time.

Taking the various temperature readings that are needed to predict and record the weather helps us build up a picture of the weather. All professional meteorologists, like the man on the right, take these readings in the same way. This is so that they can exchange and compare their data.

Temperature influences the type of weather in a place. The Sun is the driving power behind the weather. Because warm air rises and cool air sinks, the heat of the Sun stirs up the air in the **atmosphere**. This constant movement of air affects air pressure, wind, rain, and snowfall. For example, the wind is caused by air being sucked in to replace rising warm air. Different parts of the world heat up differently for lots of reasons.

Temperature influences the way we dress, the things we do and, sometimes, the safety of living things. There are many reasons why businesses need to know the temperature and the predicted temperature. For example, they need to consider how well people work in different temperatures.

Be careful!

Do not look directly at the Sun when studying the weather. Never shelter under trees during a thunderstorm, because they could be hit by lightning.

These are some of the international symbols used by weather reporters. Weather reporters try to use the same symbols so that they can understand each other's charts.

Weather symbols: clouds

■ Cloud coverage		■ General	
○	no clouds	❜	drizzle
◐	$\frac{1}{8}$ or less	•	rain
◔	$\frac{2}{8}$	• •	more rain
◓	$\frac{3}{8}$	✳	snow
◑	$\frac{4}{8}$	✳ ✳	more snow
◒	$\frac{5}{8}$	▽	showers
◕	$\frac{6}{8}$	↳	thunderstorm
◑	$\frac{7}{8}$	△	hail
●	overcast	∞	haze
⊗	sky obscured	≡	fog
		⌒	rainbow
		⌓	dew

5

The thermometer

Temperature is measured with a **thermometer**. A basic thermometer has a thin glass tube with no air in it. At the bottom of this tube is a **bulb** of liquid which expands and contracts as the temperature changes. The liquid takes up more room as the temperature gets higher and less room as the temperature drops. In most thermometers, the liquid used is coloured alcohol. Thermometers can be bought cheaply, but the more expensive the equipment is the more likely it is to be accurate.

The glass tube is mounted on a **calibrated** scale, which means that readings can be compared. There are two main scales used for measuring temperatures, called **Celsius** and **Fahrenheit**.

There are several special types of thermometer. Some are made to be placed in the ground, on the ground, or in the air. Others have special features, like ways of recording the highest and lowest temperatures over a period of time (called a minimum and maximum thermometer).

*The red liquid in the thermometer on the left is coloured alcohol. This thermometer is used for measuring normal temperatures (in your house, for example). The thermometer on the right is a minimum and maximum thermometer. **Meteorologists** use them to gather **data** which will help them forecast the weather.*

Digital thermometers

Digital thermometers can be very useful and are quite cheap to buy. Some record the highest and lowest temperatures. Others just display the current temperature. The **sensor** can be placed where you want to know the temperature, such as outside in the shade. The display unit can then be kept indoors, where it can be easily read.

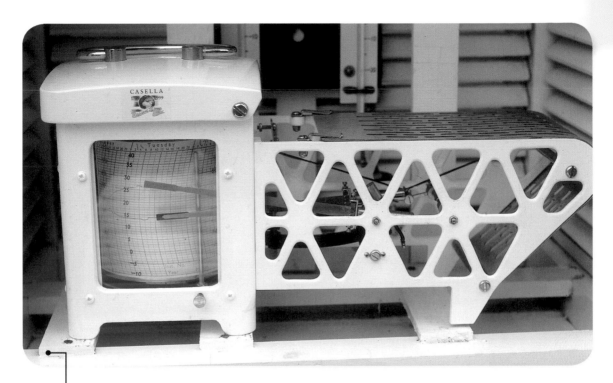

*This **thermohygrograph** measures the temperature and humidity (see page 22) continuously. It records the data on a slowly revolving chart. A special metal strip reacts to the changes in temperature. These types of instruments can record data constantly and can be used in weather stations. They are also used in museums where valuable items need to be kept in special conditions to avoid being damaged.*

BE SAFE!

- Thermometers are delicate instruments and should be handled carefully.
- Use alcohol thermometers, as mercury is very poisonous to touch if the thermometer breaks.
- Only use a thermometer for measuring temperature.

Reading the temperature

It is important that all **meteorologists** follow the same rules for reading the temperature, so that their **data** can be compared. They all read their instruments, including thermometers, at 9.00 a.m. The **thermometer** is always put at a height of 1.25 metres (4 feet) above the ground. Temperature readings always need to be taken in the shade. Professional meteorologists keep their thermometers in a special box, called a Stevenson Screen. This box shades the thermometer and also keeps it out of the wind. The thermometer can also be put on a fence in the shade. The thermometer should face north in the northern **hemisphere** and south in the southern hemisphere, so that the Sun cannot fall directly on the liquid in the thermometers. A temperature taken in this way is called the **dry temperature**. It can help to work out how much moisture is in the air.

Before reading a thermometer, check that there are no breaks in the column of liquid. This would give an inaccurate reading. To get an accurate reading, your eyes need to be level with the top of the liquid. If you look at the thermometer from above or below, your reading will be wrong.

These three pictures were taken when the thermometer was at the same temperature. Why do they all give different readings? Which one was taken from above, which from below, and which from a point level with the observer's eyes? You can find the answer on page 31.

Thermometers have a scale that is used to work out the readings. Not all of the numbers on the scale can be put on the thermometer, so you have to work out what each line on the scale represents. Work quickly when you take a reading. Your own body temperature, and breathing on the thermometer, can affect the accuracy of the reading. After you have made a reading, ask yourself if that reading is reasonable.

Using temperature data

Many people need accurate temperature readings. For example, people who make and sell food need to make sure their products are kept at the right temperatures. The colder it is outside, the easier it is to keep food products cold, and the less it will cost.

When extra electricity is needed, because of hot or cold weather, power stations need to be able to produce it quickly. Here, in the control centre, engineers work out how much electricity is needed. Monitoring the weather forecast will help them to predict how much electricity people will need.

Maximum and minimum temperatures

A maximum and minimum **thermometer** can record the highest and lowest temperatures over a period of time. The temperature rises and falls several times during the day. If the temperature is only read once a day, these changes will be missed. Using maximum and minimum thermometers may show that a warm **front**, with its warm air, has passed between readings. The minimum temperature at night is often just before dawn. This low reading would be missed if the temperature was only read at the usual time of 9:00 a.m.

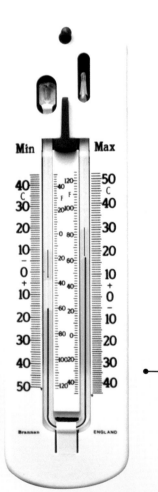

Six's thermometer

A Six's thermometer has one U-shaped tube. A liquid forces small pins upwards. These pins stay behind when the liquid falls, marking the furthest point that the liquid has reached. Its scales are not like those of an ordinary thermometer. On one side, the numbers are higher at the top and lower at the bottom. On the other side the scale is reversed (upside down). The readings are taken from the bottom of the pins.

*James Six was a keen **meteorologist**. He grew weary of getting up in the night to read the temperature! So, he invented this form of maximum and minimum thermometer.*

Once the readings have been checked, the pins are made to return to sit on the top of the measuring liquid by pressing a button, or by stroking a small magnet against the tube. The magnet attracts the metal pins down. When the thermometers have been reset, they should give readings that agree with the **dry temperature.**

14 °C
22 °C

MIN

MAX

RESET

DIGITAL THERMOMETER

Digital instruments can be used to record weather data over a period of time even when you are not there. This example can record maximum and minimum readings for both temperature and humidity. Some models have a remote sensor which can be placed a distance away from the display unit. This means that you can monitor the weather without even going outside!

Hot and cold

Depending on the amount of sunlight we get, the temperature of the air around us can be higher or lower. The amount of sunlight can vary if things like clouds get in the way. It can also vary depending on where in the world you are. Places nearer to the **equator** receive the most direct and strong rays of the Sun. The further away from the equator you get, the less strong the rays will be.

You can record the rise and fall in temperature during the day. However, the temperature recorded on one particular day cannot tell you about the **climate** in a region. To give you this information, **data** over a long period (several years) is needed. Then the data from a region can be looked at to see what the weather for each season is usually like.

Adapting to extreme temperatures

In a cold climate, people are likely to have appropriate clothes to keep them warm. In a hot climate, wearing white will reflect the heat away from your body. Architecture can tell you a lot about a region's climate. Even before air conditioning, there were ways of keeping cool. In hot countries, some buildings have tall wind towers with special **vents**, which help move air into living areas. Roofs can be built to cope with the weather. For example, in wet countries steep roofs are built so that the rainwater can run off them.

This house in Queensland, Australia is built on stilts so that air will move around and cool the house down. This is very useful in a hot climate.

TRY THIS WITH A FRIEND!

The terms "hot" and "cold" depend upon the temperature people are used to. A person living in Alaska would consider a cold day in Melbourne, Australia very warm!

Try this activity to show how the terms hot and cold can be misleading.

- Set up three bowls of water, each with a different temperature. Make one cold (10°C/50°F), one medium (25°C/77°F) and one hot (35°C/95°F).
- Ask a friend to place a hand in the bowl of cold water for a short while.
- Ask your friend to move the hand to the medium-temperature water.
- Ask them what they think the temperature is like. Repeat the process, starting with the hot water this time.

Soil temperature

Farmers and gardeners need to know the best time to plant their seeds. They do not want to waste money by sowing seeds when they will not grow. They know the best **germination** temperature for their seeds, and they check this by using a soil **thermometer** to tell them the temperature just below the surface of the soil. For example, peas germinate at a minimum temperature of 4 °C (39 °F). The farmer will wait until the soil has been this temperature for a few days before planting pea seeds.

The temperature of the soil is very different to the temperature of the air. Air temperature rises and falls quite quickly because the molecules in the air are spread out and can move about easily. This means that they can move heat about more quickly. The soil temperature changes more slowly because the soil takes longer to warm up or cool down. The deeper the soil, the slower the temperature will be to change. Longer thermometers are used to read the temperature deeper under the surface. Gardeners usually use a thermometer in a metal tube. This tube can be put in the soil so that the soil thermometer can be easily removed and read.

This farmer knows that the seeds he is planting have a good chance of growing. He has checked to see that the average soil temperature is warm enough for germination.

Deep in the soil

A deep soil thermometer shows very gradual changes in temperature. It usually shows the change in soil temperature over the seasons. A shallow soil reading will show changes in temperature during the day.

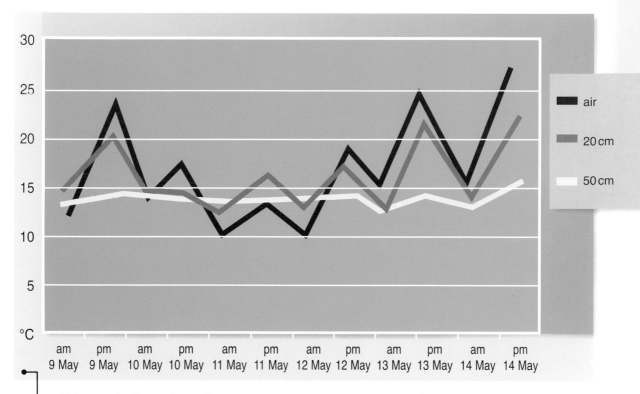

This graph shows the soil temperatures at 20 centimetres and 50 centimetres depths and the air temperature. See how the air temperature goes up and down most. Have you noticed that the temperature of the soil is different at depths of 20 centimetres and 50 centimetres?

BE ACCURATE!

- Read a soil thermometer quickly before it changes to being the air temperature!
- Do not hold the thermometer by its **bulb** or you will take your own temperature.
- Keep the thermometer out of direct sunlight when you read it (turn your back to the Sun).
- Hold the top of the liquid level with your eyes to read it.
- If water gets into your thermometer tube in the ground, use some cloth on a stick to soak it up.

Grass temperature and frost

Meteorologists place their **thermometers** 1.25 metres (4 feet) above the ground. However, the difference between this temperature and the temperature at ground level can be great. Many people need to know the ground or grass temperature. If it gets very cold, people in charge of keeping the roads clear of ice send out lorries to put grit on them. They use **digital** thermometers linked to an alarm, which goes off when it gets so cold that the roads need the grit.

Professional weather watchers use a special grass minimum thermometer. This records the lowest temperature at night by pushing a recording pin to the lowest reading. The reading is taken by looking to see what level the alcohol has pushed the pin down to. If a grass minimum thermometer is used, it needs to be set just above the level of short grass. It needs to be placed so that the **bulb** end is 2.5–5.0 centimetres (0.9–2.0 inches) above the ground, but just touching the top of the grass. Surface temperatures are always measured on grass so that **data** can be compared. If the ground temperature was measured on different surfaces, readings could not be compared. However, if there is no grass, the local soil may be used.

Sending out vehicles to spread grit onto ice is expensive. Accurate data reveals when gritting is necessary. Lives may depend on these decisions.

Frost

Sometimes, objects near the ground cool very quickly. This causes the moisture in the air to **condense**, forming tiny droplets of water called dew. When the ground cools below 0 °C (32 °F), the moisture turns directly into the powdery white crystals known as frost. Frost can damage delicate plants and weaken concrete that is setting. It is also very pretty!

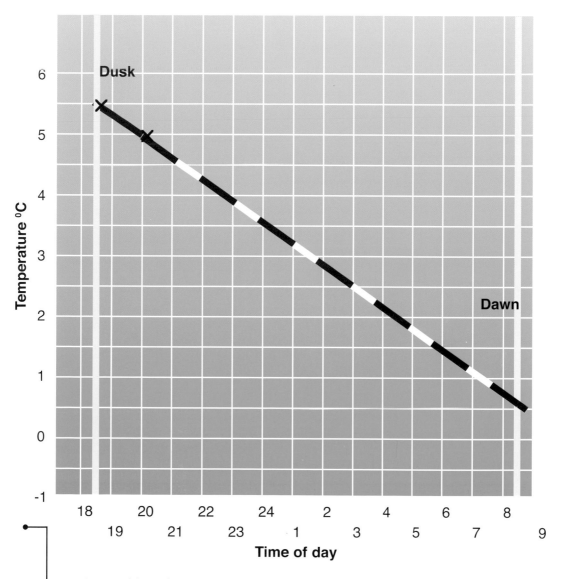

It is possible to forecast frost on a clear night if you know the times of dusk and dawn. Take the temperature just after sunset and then again about one and a half hours later. By this time the temperature should continue to fall at the same rate, unless the sky clouds over (this would make it warmer). Plot the temperatures on the graph and draw a straight line through them. Continuing the line is called extrapolating. If the line goes below zero before dawn, there will be a frost.

Sensing temperature with a computer

Maximum and minimum **thermometers** record the highest and lowest temperatures during a period of time. In between these times the temperature can go up and down and not be recorded. By using electronic devices like computers, the temperature can be constantly monitored and recorded. This helps us understand the relationship between temperature and other factors in the weather. It has the advantage of monitoring the weather without someone having to be present all of the time. This is helpful in places such as schools, because **data** can be recorded during the holidays. Computers can also be used to record weather in places that are difficult to live in, such as the Arctic or the top of mountains.

Sharing information

Many **meteorologists** have access to a **weather station** linked to a computer. This is an accurate and easy way to collect weather data. This data can be put into computer programs, such as spreadsheets and databases. The data can be used to make graphs to help predict what the weather will be like in the future. Data files can be sent digitally or even put directly onto websites using special hardware and software.

Data is collected by weather stations even in the middle of oceans, giving warnings about forthcoming weather. This means that bad weather (storms, for example) can be predicted. Weather stations like this are especially important as oceans cover 70 percent of the world!

Collecting data

Web cams can be used to view conditions around the world. You can find out a lot by looking at these pictures. For example, the clothes people are wearing can tell you about the weather in that location.

Temperature **sensors** can be used on their own or with other devices like computers. The greenhouses used to grow food and flowers need to have carefully controlled temperatures. Sensors read the temperature inside. They are linked to control units which are used to open and shut windows. So, if the temperature gets too high, the windows are opened. This cools the greenhouse down. Sensors can also control the heating and cooling systems of buildings. Buildings can have sensors that monitor temperatures and turn on the heating when there is a danger of the pipes freezing. Modern vehicles can be automatically heated or cooled depending on the outside weather conditions.

*Automatic weather stations, like this one, monitor many weather features, including maximum and minimum temperature, current temperature, **air pressure**, wind strength and direction, and humidity. They also record sunshine and wind chill. This weather station uses a solar panel to power its instruments.*

Temperature through the atmosphere

There is often a noticeable difference between the readings of a grass **thermometer** on the ground and the air around you – so imagine how different the temperature might be high up in the sky. The weather we experience only occurs in the lowest part of the **atmosphere.** Weather balloons are used to collect information about the weather in the highest points of this part of the atmosphere.

Temperature in the atmosphere is influenced by **air pressure.** The air around you has weight that presses down on everything. Although you can't feel it, the air pressure at sea level is about three times greater than at the top of Mount Everest.

Weather balloons measure the temperature and a lot of other weather **data**. They are used to build up a picture of the weather at different heights. This creates a worldwide picture of the weather. There are many weather stations around the world which release these balloons.

Layers in the atmosphere

The atmosphere is divided into several levels, which do not mix very well. The temperature at these levels varies, rising and falling, as you can see on the diagram below. The troposphere is between 10–16 kilometres (6–10 miles) thick. In this layer, all of the clouds are made, which in turn create hail, rain, snow, and thunder and lightning. This affects the temperature. In the troposphere, the temperature falls the higher up you go. Aeroplanes try to fly above the weather in the troposphere. They fly up into the next layer of the atmosphere, the stratosphere, to make it more comfortable for passengers. Crossing from the troposphere to the stratosphere can be bumpy, but once there the journey is usually smoother.

In the stratosphere, a gas called ozone absorbs energy from the Sun, and this makes the temperature go up. Although the temperature goes up, it is still very cold. Above this level is the mesosphere where the air is at low pressure, and the temperature falls again. The final layer, the thermosphere, is also known as the "hot layer". The Sun's rays warm this part of the atmosphere. Although the thermosphere goes up to about 500 kilometres (310 miles) it is very hot (2,000 °C/3,632 °F). Beyond the thermosphere is the **exosphere**.

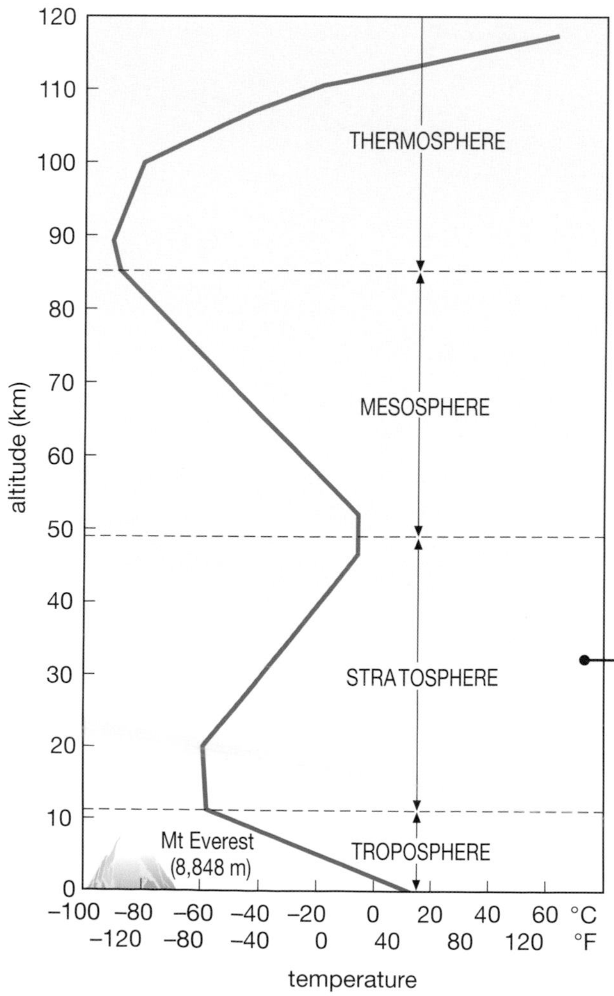

THERMOSPHERE

MESOSPHERE

STRATOSPHERE

Mt Everest
(8,848 m)

TROPOSPHERE

altitude (km)

temperature

−100 −80 −60 −40 −20 0 20 40 60 °C
−120 −80 −40 0 40 80 120 °F

The layers of the atmosphere do not go from one extreme of temperature to the other. Each layer has its own special conditions.

Humidity

Moisture is constantly escaping from rivers, lakes, the ground, and plants. Because of this, all air contains water vapour. The amount of water vapour in the air is measured as humidity on a scale from zero to one hundred and is given as a percentage. This percentage is known as relative humidity. The higher the percentage, the more water vapour is in the air. When the relative humidity is 100 percent, the air is full of water and the water vapour becomes fog.

Dew

Dew is water vapour that has condensed as the air gets cooler. It forms when the air temperature has reached "dewpoint" temperature. Even in a desert, the air is not completely dry and the water vapour in it forms dew in the evening. At night, the air cools quickly as the ground gives off the heat it has collected during the day. The water then **condenses** out of the air. Some plants in dry **climates** arrange their leaves so that they can collect this dew. This makes up for the lack of rain and means that they can survive.

The Heat Index

Our comfort is affected by the relative humidity, especially when combined with high temperatures. When the humidity is high, the temperature feels hotter than it really is. The Heat Index (HI) is used to explain this condition. People who take part in energetic sports are aware that the Heat Index can affect their performance. When selecting places to hold sports events, the organisers must consider an area's relative humidity. The table below shows how temperature and humidity affect how comfortable we feel. The Heat Index also affects how likely you are to get **heat stroke**.

How humidity makes us feel hotter			
Dry conditions (the actual temperature)	Very warm	Hot	Very hot
Humid conditions (when there is lots of moisture in the air)	Feels hot	Feels very hot	Feels extremely hot

TRY THIS YOURSELF!

It is possible to make a **hygrometer** to measure humidity. Use soft paper that can absorb moisture easily.

- Make a balance with a drinking straw threaded onto some paperclip wire and resting on a card pivot.
- Thread squares of dry paper onto one end of the straw.
- Fix a scale at the opposite end using the other end of the straw as a pointer.
- An increase in humidity will make the paper end heavier and make the pointer at the other end move up.

Wet and dry temperatures

You can find out the relative humidity by using a pair of special **thermometers** called a wet and dry bulb **hygrometer**. One thermometer has its bulb wrapped in a wet **wick**. The other thermometer is left exposed to the air. When water changes from a liquid into water vapour, it uses up energy. The energy it uses is heat. The temperature of the thermometer with its bulb wrapped in the wet wick goes down, because the water in the wick evaporates.

The difference between the temperatures of the pair of wet and dry bulb thermometers is used to work out the relative humidity. If it is a warm, dry day there will be a big difference between the wet and dry thermometers. This means the relative humidity will be low. If it is a damp day, there will be less difference. This means the relative humidity will be high.

Finding the humidity

The table below shows part of a humidity chart. To find the humidity, read the dry and then the wet thermometer, and work out the difference between the numbers. Find the **dry temperature** on the left of the chart. Then look for the difference in temperatures along the top of the chart. Read across and down from these figures to find the humidity. For example, if the dry temperature is 12 °C (i), and the wet temperature is 10.5 °C, there is a difference of 1.5 °C (ii) between the two numbers. Therefore the humidity is 84 percent (iii).

Humidity chart						
Difference / Dry Temperature	0.5 °C	1 °C	1.5 °C (ii)	2 °C	2.5 °C	3 °C
13 °C	95%	89%	84%	79%	74%	69%
(i) 12 °C	95%	89%	(iii) 84%	78%	73%	68%
11 °C	94%	89%	83%	78%	72%	67%
10 °C	94%	88%	82%	72%	71%	66%

Remember that humidity readings should fit in with the type of weather you are experiencing. This will depend on your location. Very low readings, such as 16 percent, are usually only found in deserts.

Other hygrometers

You might come across a variety of hygrometers, some modern and some older designs. Digital thermometers, like the one shown on page 11, can be used to record humidity. They can also record minimum and maximum temperatures over a period of time. A whirling hygrometer is a portable hygrometer for use away from a **weather station**. It has its own pair of matching thermometers. One of them is connected, by a wick, to a container of water. A **weather house hygrometer** has a piece of animal gut (intestines) inside the model house. It changes length when it is humid and sends out a figure with an umbrella (see the photograph below). This is meant to predict rain. A dial hygrometer is worked by human hair instead of animal gut.

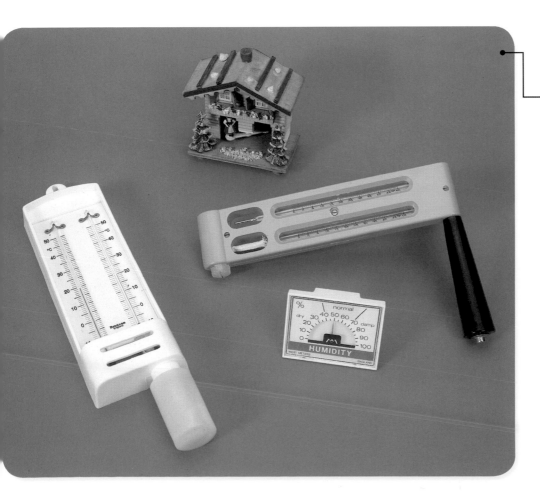

Can you tell which hygrometer is which? Use the text above to help you. The one not included in the picture is the digital hygrometer.

Cold fronts and warm fronts

When you look at a weather map of a large area, you can see very large air masses. Air masses are made up of air that contains the same amount of moisture, and is of a similar temperature. The **atmosphere** high up is made up of lots of these air masses. They start from two main places on the Earth – the very hot tropical regions and the very cold polar regions. They are always moving. If they travel over a lot of sea (maritime air masses) they pick up moisture. If they travel over a lot of dry land (continental air masses), they become drier. These air masses bring us different types of weather, depending on where the air came from and what it travelled over.

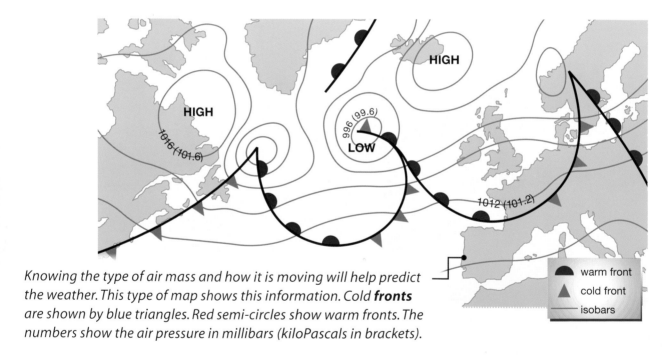

*Knowing the type of air mass and how it is moving will help predict the weather. This type of map shows this information. Cold **fronts** are shown by blue triangles. Red semi-circles show warm fronts. The numbers show the air pressure in millibars (kiloPascals in brackets).*

Where the four main air masses come from, showing what sort of weather they bring		
	Starting from polar regions (very cold)	Starting from tropical regions (very hot)
Travelled over land (continental)	Cold and dry	Hot and dry
Travelled over sea (maritime)	Cold and wet	Hot and wet

Weather maps

The main thing you will notice about a real weather map or chart is that it is covered in dark circular lines called isobars. These lines are like the **contour lines** on a map, but instead of showing height they show **air pressure**. When you see lots of lines close together, you are looking at a very windy area.

When one air mass stays still over us, the weather will be settled. If one air mass is replaced by another, the weather will change. The boundary between these two air masses is called a front. Where there are fronts, the weather is unsettled and often stormy.

A warm front is the edge of a warm air mass that is approaching a cold air mass. When the warm air mass slides over the cold air mass, various clouds appear, finishing with clouds that bring **precipitation**. A cold front is the edge of a cold air mass. It has a steep bulging edge, which produces **heaped** clouds, and often brings heavy rain as it pushes underneath a warm air mass. It gets very windy as the cold front gets nearer. A cold front also brings different clouds, sometimes ending with **cumulonimbus**.

*Air near the **equator** is hotter than air in other areas of the world. Hot air is less **dense** and rises. Cold air is denser and sinks. This starts off the movement of air in the atmosphere. The swirling clouds in this picture show this movement of air.*

Temperature and the environment

The difference in the amount of sunshine in different places means that there are clear differences in temperature around the world. Overall, the temperature near the **equator** is much hotter and the area in the polar regions is much colder. Most plants and animals live in the **temperate** and tropical areas. Life is easier in these areas. The **climate** of colder regions makes it a struggle to survive there.

The "greenhouse effect"

Lots of people are worried about the rise in temperature on the Earth. This has been named the "greenhouse effect". Certain gases in the atmosphere help to keep some of the heat that comes off the Earth from disappearing into space. But there is a balance between keeping in enough heat to keep us warm and keeping in too much heat. Some gases prevent too much heat from leaving our atmosphere. These are often called "greenhouse gases".

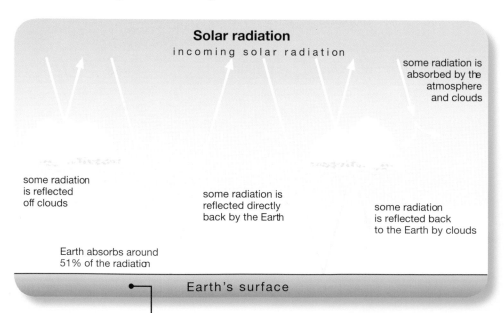

Solar radiation

incoming solar radiation

some radiation is absorbed by the atmosphere and clouds

some radiation is reflected off clouds

some radiation is reflected directly back by the Earth

some radiation is reflected back to the Earth by clouds

Earth absorbs around 51% of the radiation

Earth's surface

Heat from the Sun warms the Earth. This heat comes from solar radiation. When this heat comes off the Earth, some of it is prevented from leaving the atmosphere by 'greenhouse gases'. The difference between the heat kept and lost affects the temperature of the Earth.

Rising water levels

Some human activities may be dangerously increasing these gases. Without a change in human behaviour this will almost certainly result in a rise in temperature, which would melt the ice at the poles. Sea levels would rise and areas of low-lying land would disappear under water. This would leave less space to live in and less land for growing crops. Communities living near the sea would disappear, along with all the services they provided for the rest of the country. Most of the goods in the world are transported in ships, which need harbours where these goods can be loaded and unloaded. These harbours would disappear under the water if the sea rose.

Meteorologists are studying the way these gases are changing our weather and climate. So, measuring the weather can both help us understand the world we live in and help plan the way we live in the future.

The colours on this map show world-wide temperatures in January. The colder weather is occurring in the northern **hemisphere**. *It is summer in the southern hemisphere. These temperatures may be changing slowly.*

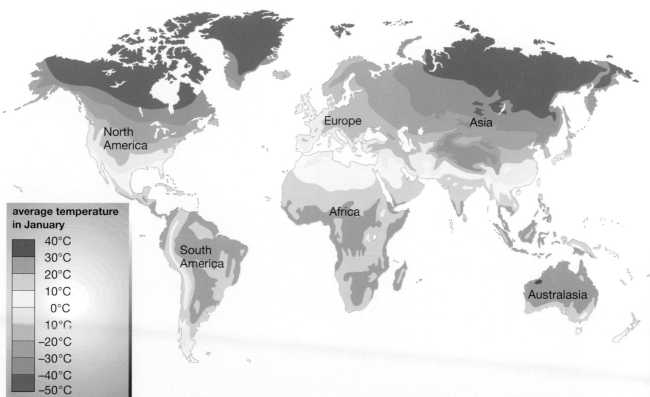

average temperature in January

	40°C
	30°C
	20°C
	10°C
	0°C
	10°C
	−20°C
	−30°C
	−40°C
	−50°C

North America

Europe

Asia

South America

Africa

Australasia

Glossary

air pressure pressure, at the surface of the Earth, caused by the weight of the air in the atmosphere

atmosphere gases that surround the planet

bulb rounded end of the glass tube of a thermometer, containing the measuring liquid

calibrated instrument which is accurately set and marked to read particular measurements

Celsius scale used in thermometers like those constructed by Anders Celsius (1701–44). In this scale, the freezing point of water is 32° and the boiling point is 212°.

climate general weather conditions of an area

condense turn from a gas into a liquid

contour lines lines drawn on a map to show the height above sea level

cumulonimbus dark, heaped cloud of great height, which often brings showers and thunderstorms

data facts that can be investigated to get information

dense thick, closely packed

digital shown as numbers or turned into data that can be understood by a computer

dry temperature temperature taken from a thermometer exposed to the air

equator imaginary line around the centre of the Earth, at equal distance from the north and south poles

exosphere highest layer of Earth's atmosphere, the one next to space

Fahrenheit temperature scale invented in 1714 by Gabriel Daniel Fahrenheit, which was used in the UK until the 1970s. In this scale, the freezing point of water is 0° and the boiling point is 100°.

front front edge of an air mass, where it meets air of a different temperature

germination the first stages of growth in a seed

heaped piled up in mounds

heat stroke illness caused by the body overheating and becoming dehydrated (not having enough water). It is common in very high temperatures.

hemisphere half of the globe, usually northern or southern

hygrometer instrument for measuring humidity, or water vapour content

meteorologist a person who studies the weather by gathering and analysing data

precipitation moisture that falls from clouds in a variety of forms, for example, rain, snow, and hail

sensor instrument for measuring a physical change, such as temperature

temperate areas that are neither too hot nor too cold

thermohygrograph instrument for recording humidity and temperature on a chart

thermometer instrument for measuring temperature

vents openings to let air in or out

weather house hygrometer toy house with two tiny people inside, a lady and a gentleman. When the lady comes out it will be dry. When the gentleman comes out it will rain.

weather stations set of weather measuring instruments placed in an appropriate location

wick specially woven piece of cloth that can pull liquid up into it

Find out more

To find out more about the climate in your area you could try to keep a long-term record of the temperature in your garden. Even recording a week's weather in each season would give some interesting data. Remember to record your temperature at the same time each day. Can you find out when professional meteorologists take their readings?

Temperature data should be collected in a special weather station. Does this really matter? Use cheap thermometers placed in different parts of your garden to record the temperature at the same time. Are the readings different? Can you suggest reasons for this?

During what months is your summer? Is it the same around the world? Use data from Weather Underground's weather data (www.wunderground.com). Choose a date in the past to research. What was the temperature like around the world on that day? Choose a place on each continent. Select the place and go to the History section. Make a note of the temperature. How much data will you need to collect to get a clear idea of the temperature zones around the world?

Websites

http://www.wunderground.com/
Weather Underground has lots of weather data and forecasts.

http://www.weatheronline.co.uk/
Click on "graphs" in the climate section to see charts of the maximum and minimum temperatures in places around the world. Look at a place in the northern hemisphere and a place in the southern hemisphere to see an interesting contrast.

http://www.amingtonheath.staffs.sch.uk/intro.html
The Staffordshire School Weather Data Site has good ideas for collecting data and for setting up your own weather station. You can also follow a link to help you build a simple weather station.

More books to read

The Usborne Internet-linked Introduction to Weather and Climate Change,
    Layra Howell (Usborne Publishing Limited, 2003)
Discovering Geography: Weather, Rebecca Hunter (Raintree, 2003)
Science on File: Weather, Richard and Louise Spilsbury (Evans, 2006)

Index